T0121802

NIGHT TO DAY

Poetry Anthology

PHATHISANI MLOTSHWA

authorHOUSE®

AuthorHouse™
1663 Liberty Drive
Bloomington, IN 47403
www.authorhouse.com
Phone: 1-800-839-8640

Published by AuthorHouse 4/17/2013

ISBN: 978-1-4817-8729-1 (sc)
ISBN: 978-1-4817-8730-7 (e)

ACKNOWLEDGEMENTS

I wish to express my sincere gratitude to the panel of my friends and the backup team that has given me all of their valuable time and patience in promptly putting this project together

DEDICATION

This book is dedicated to my ever loving wife Siphilisiwe Mlotshwa and our lovely children.

AUTHOR'S NOTE

This anthology offers a package of stories told in simple poetic language. Just like a mirror giving a true image of a person, NIGHT TO DAY portrays the joys and sorrows of a world overburdened by socio- economic and political disorientations. Cultural dreams, emotions and feelings of the ordinary African man and woman are echoed in creative imagination that makes every individual's life experiences a great treasure to draw lesson from and probably predict the future.

A quest for a better world, free from wars and problems of varying degrees acts as an undercurrent that gives the book a global appeal. It rallies men and women to a common cause-humility and empathy.

The transition from the night to a new day should see the end of most of the ills tormenting the peoples of the world, paving the way for a new world order. Therefore, let us all join the movement which advocates for a world without war, read on...

POETRY

Poetry is the spontaneous overflow of powerful feelings. Starting as a tiny spark from the dark corners of the heart, it then transforms to a blinding flash of super charged imagination.

●•●•●•●•●•●•●•●•●•●

MY LITTLE RED ROSE

Shining bright with a red glow,
With bright petals so delicate like the spongy lips of a
    damsel,
Nodding majestically to the gentle breeze,
Red rose!
You seduce my nostrils with a fragrance.
Your whole anatomy flows with sugary blood,
A sedative for bees with a sweet tooth,
My red rose you are so beautiful.
Your beauty strikes the chords of poetic language.
Sitting elegantly in a maze of thorns, you exude amazing
    confidence.
I like it when you smile to me,
Your smile is a romantic episode,
That drives me mad with passion.
They say beauty is a preserve for the beautiful,
In you beauty is what I see.

MY LITTLE SHINING STAR

On a cool summer night,
I watch my little star dancing high up in the sky.
Sailing on a sea of amazing blackness
It bathes me in a spray of shimmering light
Its glittering smile is contagious,
It leaves me with no choice- but to smile back,
Smiling that toddler smile which flashes on a child's, face when
     it sees a box of chocolates.
I like watching my little shining star,
Its magnificent sight cools my nerves
It allows my ever busy brain to take a short holiday.
Come! Sweet angel,
Stretch your arms to me
Let's dance to waltz
You and me
Under the shade of darkness,
For when dawn approaches you will be taken away from me
Fading away from sight
Like a sweet dream

I wish that one day I could fly up to you
Spend the night with a special you
See the world from above
Listen to millions of snores from millions of citizens, sleeping in
     their homes.
Worry not, my angel for one day
I will fly up to you my little shining star.

A BEAUTIFUL SUNSET

One Friday I watched a beautiful sunset by the lake side.
Sitting on a small rock facing the lake, I witnessed nature's
beauty.
The setting sun cast several glittering rays,
That spread across the horizon like the graceful arms of an
octopus,
It blended the sky with a tinge of crimson light.
The sun itself;
A red ball of fire,
Kept rolling smoothly towards the outskirts of the furthest
horizon
That was a beautiful sunset indeed!

Down where I was the placid waters reflected the beauty of
the setting sun.
The delicate rays paraded on the surface of the water
spontaneously turning it to a kaleidoscope of grandest
beauty.
Every water molecule in the lake was co-operating
in shooting a film of heavenly splendour.

(Some minutes later......)
The sun danced its last exquisite dance that signalled the end
of daylight.
Showcasing its last grin to the world it slid behind the curtains
of darkness.
The whole landscape was left in a pool of darkness.
The drama had lasted for a few minutes.
Surely, nice things in life are short-lived.

A FARMER IN BEIRUT

When the sound of thunder echoes in every valley,
Lightning illuminating the skies in summer,
A farmer in Beirut rushes to the nearest empty granary to
    hide.
For when it rains the life giving rain is usually absent,
A rain of bullets and lethal bombs is the common type.
Can rivers be replenished by blood?
Can crops thrive on a rain of bullets?
Above all life cannot exist when bullets are falling from the
    sky like rain. .

BE GRATEFUL TO GOD

God is great
God is wonderful
God is fair and just
His kindness transcends human imagination.
He commands events to happen
He is the ultimate power that rules the earth and the
heavens.

The earth is adorned with lovely roses of different types;
people, animals, vegetation and more the eye can see.
Look at the clear sparkling water flowing in the rivers,
The roaring waterfalls exploding with hydraulic power,
The gigantic blue mountains capped with feathery white
crowns of mist,
The undulating slopes drenched in bright sunlight,
The elegant sun sends its gentle and warmest touch to every
organism.
The Touch of life!
The exquisite tall trees dance to the tune of the savannah
winds, sharing the stage with the green grass.
What a sight?
Night skies are punctuated with millions of stars that send
million pools of light.
The bright moon is a sight not to be missed especially on a
cool summer night.
Crickets, owls, jackals and other nocturnal singers blend the
night with golden nocturnal hymns.
All this beauty is the simplified version of the infinite power
of God

If only we can appreciate God's power,

Humility and respect for God will multiply

Evil and sin will be washed away by the tide of righteousness.

God is great

God will always be the good God

Every sweet breath we take is just an extended offer of his kindness.

Be grateful to God.

AN EVENING WITH GRANDMOTHER

On a cold winter night,
We are gathered in grandmother's tiny hut
Outside, the frosty winds are howling and wrestling with tree
    branches.
The sky is clad in black clouds that suppress the little light from
    the half quarter moon.
Clouds of stinging dust are running across the whole plain.
Despite the chaos outside, we are warm and safe in
    grandmother's hut.
The blazing fire is sending silhouettes on the walls,
They quaver and gyrate with life
Roasting maize cobs seduce the nostrils with an amazing
    aroma, which leaves the stomach complaining
It's good to be in grandmother's hut.

Looking at us with her kind eyes, set deep in the shadowy
    sockets, she smiles at us with that ever present smile.
Her withered and wrinkled frame is the cover page for a long
    story of African struggles.
Clearing her croaky voice, she delivers the evening lectures.
It is from her hut that we are equipped with survival skills;
Cleverness, wisdom, courtesy, patience...
All lessons are offered free of charge
It is from her fireplace that we learn to live like rational
    beings
From her we learn to live in harmony
Grandmother is the fountain of wisdom
She is the spring of love.

Through her tales we see ancient people, talking in ancient
    voices.
The tales are told with great skill and humour that sharpen
    our minds with understanding
Tales of ancient people reflect great African renaissance.
Grandmother's hut is the greatest learning institute.
It abounds with streams of knowledge.

Then all of a sudden there goes – Boom! Boom!
Somebody has dropped a bomb,
The smell of burnt cordite fills the air.
We squeeze our noses trying to evade the suffocative smell.
The room vibrates with laughter
Displaying her kind smile grandmother wakes my younger
    brother who has just fallen asleep.
"Mzukulu* is your stomach upset?" asks grandmother.
Another roar of laughter ends our lecture,
We stand up and dash outside across the homestead to our
    sleeping huts.

THE AFRICAN THUNDER STORM

A battalion of protuberant, dark and angry clouds has
    gathered up on the sky.
They are packed with millions and millions of water droplets.
The earth shaking claps of thunder accompany the blinding
    flash of lighting.
The ferocious winds are wreaking havoc signifying the arrival
    of the great African storm.
The winds stop blowing,
The whole village is then draped in a blanket of noisy
    silence,
Everyone is itching with anxiety,
For the rain is good and fearsome.
People have barricaded themselves in their huts.
Occasionally the elders cast quick glances knitted with fear
    out through their windows.
For the life giving rain has finally come.
With one final growl of thunder,
The individual water droplets pelt the ground at different
    intervals.
At last the heavens break loose,
Silvery sheets of solid rain descend on the whole country side.
"Woza malamulela!*"- The people shout from their houses
    with joy.
The rain has come to extinguish the wicked flames of drought.
Soon the whole countryside will be transformed to picturesque
    splendour.
The spell of good health will re-incarnate the people.
Oh! How great it is, the life giving rain.

BROKEN MIRROR

When man was born,
The world saw the immaculate image of God.
The moment evil thoughts crossed his mind,
He became a broken mirror.

SMILE

When the path of life turns to be rocky
Your roads narrowing dangerously
The vast waters of your life turning turbulent
Volcanoes of trouble ejecting red hot cinders of misery
Gallons of stress, stressing you
Dews of hope evaporating
High powered exhaustion driving you
Propelled by impatience
Losing your grip
Insanity insulting your sanity
Daylight turning to darkest nights
Take a break...
A good break,

Take your time,

A good time,

Do not hurry,

Close your eyes
Breathe deeply
Then smile your best smile
Let it be a good smile,
Better than that of a teddy bear.

Watch out for the results,
The world will smile back at you.

THE RICH ONLY GIRLS HIGH

In the school basket ball court school girls are playing.
They are a fine pack of robust kids, bubbling with
    happiness.
They are CAREFREE-E-E-E!
Raging with agility,
Smiles are flashing on the bright faces
Their shiny cheeks and full bodies tell the great tale of good
    health.

One tall and slim girl darts across the pitch,
Tactfully she guides the ball with her fine sculptured fingers.
From the other side of the court,
There emerges an exploding bulky figure of a girl.
Mocking her gigantic size, fast speed propels her to snatch
    the ball from the slim girl.
At the blink of an eye the whole pitch explodes into a frenzy
    of excitement.
The other team has scored the winning goal
Two minutes later the coach signals the end of game.
The players simply vanish from the court in a cloud of
    excitement.
One by one they get into their parents' cars,
Some get in their own cars.
Fine models of sophisticated technology;
BMWs, Mercedes, Toyota...

Across the street an almost indistinct figure resembling a
    human being is leaning on a pole.
Gazing with tear full eyes,

A homeless, fatherless, motherless child,
Watches the scene with great pains of regret,
Her name is Ragamuffin,
She is clad in filthy and tattered clothes
Poor child!
Brine tear drops blur her field of vision.
She then decides to seek comfort in her "house"
A pungent and nose shrinking storm drain
If only she could...
If only she was...
If only somebody could...
To people like her wishes will always be a haunting fairy
    tale.

A CHILD

A child is innocent
It knows no guilt
You carry it in your arms you become good friends
When you do well it admires you
When it smiles, the smile is genuine.
A child is a wonderful thing
When the child does something wrong you slap it on the cheek
And it cries.
You give it ice-cream, it smiles.
A child knows no grudges
Its tiny heart is always ready to forgive
A child is a great blessing to every parent.

GOD BLESS ZIMBABWE

Strategically wedged between two mighty rivers,
The great Zambezi and the magnificent Limpopo,
There lies a sacred land called Zimbabwe.
Treasure of great natural wonders,
The thundering Victoria -Falls exhibiting megatons of aquatic
    splendour.
The Matopos, home of the sleeping giants- Fascinating granite
    formations.
The sun drenched Eastern Highlands stretching their necks
    towards heavens.
Land of the great ancestors
Mother of many tribes living in symbiotic harmony,

May God send his life giving rains to our great country
May He calm down the raging seas of hunger wreaking
    havoc in the great Nation
Let the Almighty send the vicious storms of economic crises to
    the never come back lands.
Let the great nation return to its glamour as the land of milk
    and honey.
Zimbabwe is a great nation, land of good opportunities.

Let the long nights of nightmares and horrors pass away into
    annals of history.
Let a new day bring hope and joy to all the people of
    Zimbabwe.

WAITING IN VAIN

It was 10pm on Friday,
The factory labourer had knocked off from a tedious shift
His eagerness to be home, propelled him homewards
He whistled an old familiar tune,
His right hand was clutching his monthly blessings, fruits of
   back breaking labour.
It was two more streets before he got home.
Tonight he greatly missed his flamboyant wife and children
On paydays life at home was like honeymoon.
He came across a dark alley.
His eyes partially noticed three shadowy figures sticking to
   one of the walls,
Suddenly, the shadows sprang to life,
A shining object struck him on the head,
His whole anatomy vibrated with great pounds of pain,
Tonight he will never reach home...
In seconds he became a crumpled figure lying in a pool of
   blood.
Why was life so unfair?

At home the wife kept looking at her watch.
Poor wife!
Already a widow,
Tonight the waiting shall be forever.

WAGES OF SIN

On a hot and bright afternoon,
A black Mercedes was speeding to an out of town
    destination,
It was a fine piece of metal with a silent engine and grand
    appearance.
That was a car indeed!

The occupants were smartly dressed,
Man in formal attire- woman in modern fashion.
BUT...
Something was terribly wrong.
Despite the supersonic speed they were travelling at, they
    were enveloped in a small world of passion.
Momentarily the driver took his eyes off the road and received
    a blood heating kiss from the woman.
Simply he went berserk overpowered by passion and desire.
Streaks of grey hair explained that the man was old enough
    to be the girl's father.
What an abomination!
She was only a sweet sixteen.
The man had a loyal wife at home
Poor wife!

The vehicle approached a blind curve.
Tyres smoked.
There was a loud screeching of brakes,
The car slipped over the edge of the road and disappeared
    in a very large cloud of dust.

Some minutes later the car lay on its side against a large
   boulder.
It became a complete wreckage of twisted metal and broken
   glass.
The mutilated bodies of the lovers had been thrown out of
   the car.
Blood was everywhere, quenching the thirst of the hot and
   dry soil.
Some kind of an offering to the gods,

Not far away from the man's body was his brief case lying
   open, the contents had been strewn all over the grass.
Amongst those was a small Bible.
Out of nowhere a light breeze flipped the pages of the small
   Bible,
A marked verse appeared,
                    "For the wages of sin is death"
As if by magic the man's head rose,
His pain covered eyes landed on the Bible.
Something seemed to ignite in those fading eyes,
But it was too insignificant to make history.
He expelled a low and prolonged breath,
Without further adieu, he sped to meet with his creator.

THE BUTTERFLY

You see it dancing on a flower to an inaudible beat.
Its slender legs resemble those of a ballet dancer
Dressed in a powdery garment of beautiful colours
It simply watches the harsh world go by.
What a free creature?

Its world is a calm one existing within a strange and cruel
one.
The small world continues to thrive unaffected by a world of
sorrow, misery, deaths, pains and wars.
A butterfly knows no talk about climate change or global
warming.
To a butterfly ignorance is bliss.
Go on, fly my butterfly!
Let the flap of your wings echo the sound of hope and a
breath of a new life.

THE VAGABOND

He sat at the corner of the street, puffing black clouds of
cigarette smoke into the air.
From time to time spasms from a violent cough jerked his frail
body,
In spite of all that he continued to suck hard on a large block
of street made cigarette.
His eyes were hot ambers focussed in space, seeing an
invisible picture,
Filthy rags barely covered his body coated with black grease
of dirt.
Nobody cared to go near him.
Poor man! A lonely figure indeed,
A squadron of flies buzzed over his head singing a buzzing
lullaby to their friend.

He last ate a piece of rotten sadza centuries ago.
Life on the street was tough but at least he was "free"
Free from any kind of responsibility.
He did not desire to waste his time working for other greedy
men.

From his vantage point he just watches the world go by,
To him life is just a barren landscape.
He stopped living a decade ago,
He once had greater dreams for a bright future.
Now he is just a living zombie.
He is a dirty spot on a cloth of humanity.

The sound of streaming traffic does not even perturb him.

To him civilisation is a piece of human mischief.

To the human race he is a great reminder of the unpredictable
life, hanging over their heads.

THE JUICE OF WISDOM

My cup is full to the brim, with thick boiling tea.
Soluble sands of sugar melt into an amazing sweetness.
Creamy milk transforms my tea to a creamy affair.
Stirring it with my teaspoon it turns to a whirlpool of tongue
    tickling sweetness.
Tea is delicious.

Without tea life is pregnant with boredom.
Tea makes the world go round
Men have a boiling passion for tea
Women have an itching desire for tea.
Tea is delicious.

On cold winter nights in my study room,
Engaged in serious data blasting,
Writing mountains of manuscripts,
Tea is my fuel.
It stimulates my powerful mind.
It adds to my wisdom.

It takes an entire tiresome planting season to harvest a grain
    of tea
Yet it takes barely five seconds to ignite my mind with
    wisdom.
Tea is for the wise.
With a cup of tea on your hand,
You have the world in your hands.

THE SECURITY GUARD

He guards his employer's premises with great care and vigilance.
Meticulously and inexorably, he protects his employer's property from thieving hands.
On very cold nights, he is a lonely shadow nearly freezing to death patrolling the premises.

His presence instils peace on the employer's mind.
He is a great peace keeper.
Nothing can outwit his watchful eye armed with acute night vision,
He can even spot ants mating on the dark walls surrounding the premises.
His ears can even pick the faint footsteps of a lizard darting across the lawn.
In his profession there is no such thing as a good night sleep.
At night he is most active,
The employer's riches are totally under his custody.
He owns them,
Very rich by night
By day they are taken away from him,
Very poor by day

On pay days he is mostly stressed.
His payslip is a great mockery on his splendid work.
When I saw his payslip one day, I fainted several times.
The payslip is thinner than a starving old lady.
No words can describe what I saw,
To say he earns peanuts will be a great understatement,
For he always receives peanut shells.

HOPE

Hope is a wonderful thing.
It keeps us going every day,
Hope brings courage
Perseverance streamline's one's vision
Hope replenishes all energy levels.

Solid hope clears barriers of uncertainty.
With hope impossibilities are transformed to possibilities.

On the very darkest nights, hope is like a small star dancing
    at the top of High Mountain.
Casting a silvery thin strip of light it glitters like a distant city.
Its mere presence is a sign that dawn is not far away,
With hope dreams turn to reality.
Hope is a wonderful thing.

THE GOSSIPER

He spends a lot of valuable time talking about other people.
Backbiting and poking his bulbous nose into other people's
    affairs,
Always criticising and failing to see good in others.
His life is a busy one.
Always harbouring evil thoughts,
Spreading rumours and fuelling conflicts.
Powered by jealousy and driven by ignorance

At old age others proudly look at their greatest achievements,
The gossiper has no medals to show for his "greatest
    achievements."
His friend's children have wealth to inherit.
The gossiper has nothing to pass on to his children.
He blames everything on misfortune and lack of opportunity,
He is bitter against every one.
Regret is a pension for a gossiper.

VIRTUOS WOMAN

I nearly spent all my life looking for a virtuous woman.
A woman with a soft heart like wool whose mouth over flows
     with wisdom.
A woman who wears a veil of fidelity,
A paragon of virtue

Through large villages and hamlets,
I met many beautiful girls.
I was no fool to accept any of them as a wife to marry.
Like numerous pairs of reflectors, their eyes reflected deceit
     embedded in their heads.
They greeted me with lopsided smiles, a true replica of
     cunningness in them.
None of those imposters of beauty could win my heart.
I continued with my long search,
I kept wondering,
What happened to faithful women?

Many summers passed, but still my prayers had not been
     answered.
With a weather beaten face I faced the chilly winters that
     threatened to tear me apart.
Stumbling and staggering on rocky terrain, I maintained my
     pace.
I could not turn my back now. Never!
It would be a disgrace if I abandoned my search.
Shreds mottled with dirty, represented my once beautiful
     coat.

What was once my shinny wellington boots could not qualify
    to be owned by a pauper,
Many sleepless nights elapsed,
Yet, I could not find a true woman.
Like birds of the same feather, all women were the same.
Desperation and despondency finally caught up with me.
The strength in my legs vanished.
The legs grew stiff and stubborn, refusing to take orders from
    me.
I could not bear this anymore...
Under the cool shade of a willow tree, I slipped into the dark
    corridors of sleep...

As I emerged from the dungeons of sleep an angel had fallen
    from the sky.
I gapped at the strange presence not believing my luck after
    all my troubles.
There-e! In front of me stood a woman!
As she paraded exhibiting her sculptured beauty, I missed
    my breath.
She wore a scintillating smile so powerful it could erase evil
    thoughts on a sorcerer's mind.
Behind her enticing bosom, a heart of gold overflowing
    with sympathy and kindness kept beating sending shock
    waves of love.
The woman excelled descriptions of any kind.
Clutching me with tender hands of love, she helped me onto
    my feet and off we went....
Off we went to establish our kingdom with my new found
    queen.
I had found a woman!

Every rising sun brought celebrations to our kingdom.
Every hour strengthened our love for one another.
Every ticking minute knitted strings of trust.
Every second locked our castle gates, keeping treachery and
    deceit at bay.
For I had found a true woman,
A woman with a heart of gold,
That was my virtuous woman.

WHAT DEATH CANNOT DO

Death is the greatest enemy of mankind.
An inevitable visitor in every home,
A non- discriminatory enemy,
The fair skinned,
Dark skinned,
The rich and the poor,
Man, women and children shudder and tremble at the thought
of death,
Death is unpredictable,
It strikes where it is least expected.
Cruel indeed!
Many have died and many shall die.

Super models have failed to ignore the horn of summon,
Great philosophers and statesmen have deserted large
volumes of books and air conditioned rooms, to dine
with death in windowless rooms.

It is the greatest magician,
Its diabolic and evil spell turns happiness to sorrow.
A great monster with an insatiable appetite,
There is no cruelty higher than death itself.
The more we try to run away the more we get closer to
death.
What a paradox?
Death is as ugly as death.

No matter how indestructible death is,

No matter how daring it is,

No matter how skilful it is,

There is only one superior thing death cannot erase - GOOD DEEDS!

Good deeds are an indelible ink etched on the face of humanity.

DAY DREAMS

It was the last lesson of the day,
The teacher kept preaching a history sermon to a bunch of
    tired and bored pupils.
One school boy kept dozing at the back of the class, lulled
    by the teacher's voice.

Suddenly, he had turned to a rich businessman,
Holidaying in Cape Town,
With a girl from his class whom he always had a crush on,
They were sun bathing on the beach drinking ice cold orange
    juice.

When he came around, he had become a pop star, thrilling
    large crowds with his golden voice in London.
Behind the stage, a limousine was waiting to transport him to
    one of London's finest hotels.

Quickly, he caught a plane to Hollywood,
He was featuring in an action movie,
Jean Claude Van Damme was his partner.
They were fighting a group of gangsters, walloping them with
    their fine martial arts.

At the blink of an eye he beat time at the speed of light.
He found himself in Cyber Sunday,
Watching the great fight between his favourite wrestlers-John
    Cena and Randy Orton.
Still excited by the fight, the boy received a soft nudge on
    the shoulder.

Somebody asked a question,
> "Who was King Mzilikazi's first son?"

Not caring less, he shouted,
"Cyber Sunday."

Slowly the dream ended.
He was back in class,
Everyone was giggling with laughter,
He could not understand why.
Then his body was gripped with shock as he saw the altered
        figure of his ever smiling teacher.
The teacher's face was puffed up in anger,
His whole frame shook with rage,
The eyes resembled the red traffic lights.
The school boy slowly understood the situation......

DEATH OF A MURDERER

Everyone came to witness it.
The village square was packed to full capacity,
Everyone itched to witness the killing of a murderer.
The man whose hands were red with innocent victim's blood
The blood that screamed for revenge,
The man was a threat to the human race.
The jury had declared.
He deserved to die!
Everybody sang the song,
   "Kill him! Chop off his head!"
    "Kill the murderer!"
The slogan echoed across the square.
Everyone was dancing with great excitement,
One could mistake the hullabaloo for a wedding
 celebration.
Everyone was happy.
The murderer was going to be beheaded.
The monster himself wore an unconcerned look.
He towered over the executioners who tied him to the frame
 of the guillotine.
His eyes were seeing what no canal sight could see.
He was very calm
He listened to the slogans being chanted with surprising
 equanimity.

Slowly the blade descended aimed for his neck.

Every motion of the blade fuelled the thunderous roar of excitement.

At long last the blade reached its destination- The murderer's neck.

The sound was a like a butcher's chug. The head fell on the grass,

The body twitched a few times in reflex.

Blood was everywhere.

The monster had been exterminated.

His cold and limp body explained the completion of the whole exercise.

BUT suddenly.........

No longer were the people happy,

The whole square had been plunged into an abyss of silence.

A chill of sadness gripped every participant.

Why now?

Everyone's heart nearly froze with pity,

The blood in their veins nearly coagulated.

They began to understand life....

Death does not cleanse death.

To kill even a murderer is sin.

The death of a murderer had turned everyone to a murderer

He had killed, they had killed.

GREATEST CARE GIVER

Woman! Mother of a nation,
Symbol of pride
Greatest caregiver the world has ever known.
You are great, Greater than greatness.

Wise men and great statesmen once suckled from your
breast.
The burning spirit of bravery running in the soldiers' veins was
heated a long time ago by your nutritious elixir- milk.
You give birth to man and later to love man.
Woman! You are great.

Kings give birth to kingdoms,
Women give birth to Kings.
Come on woman! Arise I say,
Clamour for your rights.
You deserve your dignity.
Gone are the days, when women were marginalised.
The world for men, and domesticity for women,
We say YES to women empowerment.
We say YES to economic emancipation of women.

Above all, we say YES to the upholding of women's rights for
the benefit of the whole society.

CHANGE

When the seed starts to decay, germination gives birth to a
new plant rippling with life.

When a once strong idea starts fading away, a new one
has just availed itself.

When a melodious song degenerates to a common jingle, a
new and refined one has just been composed.

When a visitor overstays his welcome, a more distinguished
visitor has just arrived.

When a once bright generation is snuffed out by age, a new
generation has just emerged to do even greater things.

Change is a great force.
Those who resist change will in turn be changed by change.

THAT SIMPLE AND HAPPY LIFE

The winds are blowing gently,
The morning sun casts warm rays that lick the morning dew.
Weaver birds are singing the good morning chorus.
Blue smoke from cooking fires can be seen rising high up in
     the sky,
The whole countryside reflects that simple and happy life,
It is a life of peace and tranquillity.

In the homestead it's a hive of activity.
The old farmer is milking his only cow,
Whistling an old tune, his mind goes back to his exciting years
     of youth,
That was then...
His wives are busy smearing cow dung on the mud floors, the
     amazing African floor polish.
In one of the huts, a large pot is sitting gracefully on the fire.
Breathing hot steam in a low pitched whistle, it is full with
     African delicacies.
Outside not far away, young children are playing excitedly,
Periodically they scratch their bare and shinning posteriors,
     not caring less about their nudity.
They are free spirits.
The great African cubs!
At the far end of the homestead chickens are scratching the
     dark earth for worms.
The country side is an emblem of that simple and happy life.

In the plain a large dust cloud signifies the approaching army
of head boys.
They are driving their heads to the green pastures.
The head boys are tough young men with gleaming muscles.
Their sight sets the milk boiling in young maiden's breasts,
Soon the young men will grow up to be responsible
husbands.

In the nearby river young girls are fetching water.
They are chattering excitedly, telling each other about their
lovers.
Their chocolate bodies are wet, shimmering from the morning
swim.
African angels, I tell you!
The sight of their strong and intact breasts drives a spell of
passion into the boys.
Soon they will grow up to be responsible mothers.

In the fields, the villages are tilling the land, for the rains are
just a stone's throw away.
In the afternoon when it gets very hot, they will sit in the
shade and drink "mahewu*", a cold and refreshing African
drink.
Tales will then be told to eager listeners.
Burning issues will be discussed before the last lap of the
work is covered.
Oh! How good it is to be in the country?

KINDNESS

Kindness is a great virtue.
A great cousin of compassion,
Kindness fosters truth,
It is rich in empathy.

Kindness is a Devine gift,
A great vine yard of wisdom,
Kindness thrives on good thoughts,
Good thoughts prolong life.
Kindness embodies all the Ten Commandments,
The afflicted find an everlasting cure in kindness.
The meek appreciate acts of kindness.
The starving are fed to unfathomable satisfaction in
    kindness,

Kindness is a gently breeze of goodness, easily acceptable
    to the loving and caring.
If all people were driven by kindness;
There would be no such things as the Middle East crisis,
The endless wars in the world,
Political unrest,
Religious squabbles,
Discrimination- by race, tribe, region and class
Treachery,
The list is endless...

If all were kind, the world would be a better place to be.
Kindness is found lacking in the world of today,

CAT AND MOUSE GAME

They are scattered on the dusty sodden streets
Yelling and screaming to passers by
Some even grab the passersby, by their garments.
Watch out! They can even block your way
Do not mistake them for a terror squad
They are in business
Real business
Cardboard boxes full of fruits and vegetables, explain the
    nature of their business.
Today business is good
Boxes are emptying fast.
They prefer to earn their income through enterprising means
Their industry has the power to sustain their families
But their firm is illegal
They have a problem there.

Suddenly, the whole place plunges into deep chaos.
Everyone is sprinting for cover
Loud whistling fuels the whole web of pandemonium
Strange choruses filter through the air,
A jargon only understood by the "mice"
There is too much running around for one to understand.
All the mice scamper for cover, running at a supersonic
    speed
In this business speed and alertness is a pre-requisite.
Most of the entrepreneurs hold a Bachelor of Science in
    "*Speedology.*"
Seconds later, it becomes clear as to why everyone is in
    flight.

The Big "cats" have arrived
Half a dozen "mice" are caught
The goods confiscated
The culprits are taken to the cats' den where a fine for illegal
	peddling greatly awaits them.

Ten minutes later they are back on the streets.
Doing business as usual
This game is now part of their everyday life.
This exciting game provokes sympathy and it leaves the
	desperate still desperate.

WHEN PEACE REIGNS

When peace reigns there is peace.
All noble humanity is at peace when there is peace.
Peace is the resultant force of the love for all mankind.
They say love loves,
I say peace is peaceful.

When peace is at the throne,
All humble subjects are at peace,
True peace guides all flock to the truth
It is a great compass,
That leads to the rivers of life.
The worthiness of peace is marked by its attachment to the
    truth,
Is it not a great virtue?

THE MYSTERY OF LOVE

Has always been there
Was there
Will be there
Always a mystery
Changing colours
Shedding its skin now and then
Yet remaining love,
Sweet love,
Hateful love,
Graceful love,
Comprehend able,
Puzzling...

To the righteous, love is light
To love is to live,
To a sinner, love is darkness
Love is sin.

Love constructs,
Love destroys
Love is painful
It is a metaphor for all reality.

An invisible force with a visible touch,
An intangible power with tangible results,
From a multitude of faces of love there is only one genuine love.
Love for all
That alone is love
It links us with the most cherished day of creation.

THE DAILY BREAD

A morning prayer recited by little Susan's family every
    morning.
> "Give us this day our daily bread..."

She always wondered,
No matter how hard they prayed,
There was no bread to eat.
The shelves in the shops were always empty.
Occasionally, she would spot their rich neighbours carrying
    loaves of bread,
Bought somewhere with large sums of money
Where did they get theirs from and how?
She was too young to know...

One day she will learn the sad story and live it through.
Meanwhile, she was a new character in the story of the daily
    bread.

THE VISION

It came as a nightmare,
Inescapable,
Terrifying,
I could not shake it off my mind,
Very clear and bright as the midday sun.

I saw myself suffering,
Lost on the dark avenues of life,
I staggered on uneven grounds of misery,
Tumbling into pits of uncertainty,
I tried to climb up the ladder,
Victory beckoned me to the top
Success seemed like a distant glow in the horizon.
I was the rich men's ladder to eternal glory.

The vision was an unpalatable reality,
Bitter soup
Amid all the suffering I struggled to create a life,
My life
Better life
I took the oath,
"Struggle until victory"

After years of great torment by the dewy cold
I found myself sleeping in a mansion.
Great men became my friends,
I was different,
I also mingled with the downtrodden
A hen knows it came from the egg.

REMINISCENCES OF SLAVERY

Slavery was the darkest hour in human history,
A period of doom and gloom
A time when human dignity was thrown to an abyss of
    savageness,
The perilous night, unforgotten by generations to come
A period of great lamentation in the annals of history
Now that is history.
Let bygones be bygones.

BUT...Slavery becomes a monstrous apparition of cruelty
    when the liberated race fails to liberate its self through
    engaging in good deeds.
When it becomes a danger to itself
When it enslaves itself through lack of compassion,
When it oppresses itself by failing to discard nightmares of the
    yesteryears of turmoil,
Above all, when the liberated continue to live in the past while
    fumbling with the present.

SONG OF UNBORN CHILD

Dearest mother I know you love me.
Every minute I hear your joyful heart beating with great
    anticipation.
Your musical thoughts are like the sound of a violin,
To me it is a different case.

I dread to think about the day of my birth.
A day I will embark on a tedious march to humanity,
The end of nine months of paradise,
Fear and more fear is what I feel every passing day.
Soon I shall be entering a sterile world,
A new world, old world
A world that has outlived its life span,
A world that has seen better days,
A world on the brink of decay
A world covered with numerous ills.
Once a beautiful world still a beautiful world but...

RAPE VICTIM

She was a little girl
An innocent child,
Her veins flowed with youthful blood.
What a lovely rose she was.
Her beauty glowed like the morning star.
With soft horns jutting from her chest
When they brushed a man's chest,
The victim went berserk.
She was a free spirit, a dove hovering on the azure sky.

Then he came on the picture of her life.
The beast,
Vile animal,
The Rapist
Once a trusted family friend
He enticed her to join him in his wonderland.
Another Alice in Wonderland

Suddenly, they were lost in a stormy sea,
Beauty and the beast,
The two of them sailed in a tiny boat,
Great waves were tossing the boat,
This way and that
The boat had no tiller
Each to and fro motion banged their bodies on the walls of
	the weird boat.
Every motion sent daggers of painful pleasure through her
	fragile body.
A school of great waves sent the boat bobbing up and down.

The sky was draped in a cloak of darkness.
She was scared!
He was smiling wickedly
She yearned to be home.
Home seemed not to exist.

After what seemed like eternity, the nightmare ended.
She was back in her room,
A worn out vessel she became,

Now alone in her room, guiltiness is chewing her,
She is very ill.
Nervous breakdown,
Depression,
His image on her mind torments her,
It is an apparition mocking her from the dark corners of her
    room.
For how long will she keep quiet?
Silence is lethal,
One day the membrane of silence will break.
She will have to talk, and talk she will.

GREAT RACE

Life is a great race
From the cradle we are keen to explore world.
The world is bright.

Second Lap
The proving grounds
The adolescent stage makes the world look even brighter
No worries about tomorrow.

Third Lap
The Joy or Crisis stage
Marriage brings joy and problems
The world is either complete or broken.
Fourth Lap
Evaluation stage
Old age makes us realise the truth about ourselves.
The world begins to be a lonely place

The Final Lap
Death is the concluding chapter
The world ceases to be of any significance.

A DROP OF BLOOD

The sacred liquid
The drop of blood is the relic of the lost world
It is a great link between the present and the future.

Above all, it is the code of interconnectedness.

CRIES OF THE BLACK GENE

Africa the dark continent
Cradle of human kind
The richest continent
The poorest of them all,

We were once a people with a culture
A pride of our ancestors
Having our own indigenous knowledge systems
Wisdom and virtue were our guiding principles
We were once a people with a vision.
But alas!
We allowed other nations to dismantle our chain of
    existence
We were carried away by the tide of delusion
We threw away our African ways,
They were archaic,
Barbaric,
Uncivilised,
So we were made to believe
We became a people with no culture
Cultural beggars we became,
Begging to be foreigners in their motherland
Identity crisis set in,
We could no longer define ourselves
We were reduced to little mimic men and women imitating
    foreign cultures
Caught in a web of ignorance

Africa arise, you are lagging behind,
People of Africa unite!
While you are engaged in political squabbles,
Other nations are inside their big laboratories coming up with
    greatest inventions
Wars are mushrooming every- where.
Brothers and sisters are busy pointing fingers to one another
Great kingdoms are collapsing every day.

People of Africa, let's face the music
It's time to cast away chains of yesteryears,
Let's not be victims of our own jungle mentality,
Let's not be a danger to our selves.
Do we want other nations to protect us, from ourselves?
We are children born from the same womb -Africa.
Time is not on our side
We need to start building a future for our children.
We need to bandage the wounds of the past,
We have everything at our disposal
Who said we cannot invent things?
The time is past, for us to be the major importers of foreign
    inventions.
We are tired of living on hand outs,
Let's work!
Change is what we need
It is in us
Like the humble bee,
Let's work together
Like the humble ant,
Let's live in harmony.

SPARK OF THE IMAGINATION

Greatness springs from the imagination.
Starting as a tiny spark, later it explodes to a blinding flash of
    intelligence and knowledge.

Great life changing inventions were once wishful thinking until
    somebody took the initiative to bring them to life

As you sip your coffee today look around, most of what
    you see once got somebody into trouble for wishing for
    something that did "not exist."

Imagination! The superior weapon,
You imagine something later it exists.
What a spell?
What have you imagined and brought to life?
I imagined sharing my views with the world- I wrote a book.
What have you imagined?

NIGHT TO DAY

The fiery night seemed longer than any other night,
Screams and cries of terror split the eerie night.
Greediness turned men to wolves.
Deadly fire works illuminated the darkest night ever.
The night of doom!

Suicide bombers expressed their discontent by blowing little
    children to smithereens.
Was it all in the name of Truth and Justice?
Bombs fell like rain drops flooding the whole landscape in a
    tidal wave of misery, great pain and death.
Army tanks streamed through the streets like common traffic
    during the peak hour.
Army regalia became the common attire.
That was the fiery night.

...Now we have entered a new day
Different day,
There has been enough bloodshed in the whole world.
Let's join hands and sing a song of peace,
Battle fields should be turned to dance floors.
Let's dance together and create a routine of togetherness.
Let the sound of guns be turned to beats of joy.
Turn army uniforms to garments of peace.
Turn army tanks to water tanks and send them to drought
    prone jungles of Africa.
Fears of the night should be over and joys of the day should
    prevail.
We have moved from night to day.

A world without war is possible.

MEANINGS OF NON ENGLISH WORDS CONTAINED IN THIS ANTHOLOGY.

The following words have been derived from the Ndebele language which is one of the official languages spoken in Zimbabwe.

Mzukulu	- means grandson
Woza malamulela	- means come rain, a song normally sung by children when the rains start falling as a way of expressing joy and happiness
Mahewu	-a delicious drink made from sorghum meal. Elders normally prefer this type of drink after completing a labour taxing task in the fields on a very hot day